Up from the Ashes:
Rebuilding Japan after World War II

Titles in the series include:

LUCENT LIBRARY *of* HISTORICAL ERAS

UP FROM THE ASHES:
REBUILDING JAPAN AFTER WORLD WAR II

PATRICIA OHLENROTH

LUCENT BOOKS

An imprint of Thomson Gale, a part of The Thomson Corporation

THOMSON

™

GALE

Detroit • New York • San Francisco • New Haven, Conn. • Waterville, Maine • London

LIBRARY OF CONGRESS CATALOGING-IN-PUBLICATION DATA

Ohlenroth, Pat.
  Up from the Ashes : Rebuilding Japan after World War II / by Pat Ohlenroth.
    p. cm. -- (Lucent library of historical eras. Twentieth-century Japan)
  Includes bibliographical references and index.
  ISBN 978-1-4205-0028-8 (hardcover)
  1. Japan--History--1945---Juvenile literature. I. Title.
  DS889.O253 2007
  952.04--dc22
                                                         2007030620

ISBN-10: 1-4205-0028-7
Printed in the United States of America

Contents

◆

Foreword

Looking back from the vantage point of the present, history can be viewed as a myriad of intertwining roads paved by human events. Some paths stand out—broad highways whose mileposts, even from a distance of centuries, are clear. The events that propelled the rise to power of Germany's Third Reich, its role in World War II, and its eventual demise, for example, are well defined and documented.

Other roads are less distinct, their route sometimes hidden from view. Modern legislatures may have developed from old tribal councils, for example, but the links between them are indistinct in places, open to discussion and interpretation.

The architecture of civilization—law, religion, art, science, and government—as well as the more everyday aspects of our culture—what we eat, what we wear—all developed along the historical roads and byways. In that progression can be traced every facet of modern life.

A broad look back along these roads reveals that many paths—though of vastly different character—seem to converge at a few critical junctions. These intersections are those great historical eras that echo over the long, steady course of human history, extending beyond the past and into the present.

These epic periods of time are the focus of Historical Eras. They shine through the mists of history like beacons, illuminated by a burst of creativity that propels events forward—so bright that we, from thousands of years away, can clearly see the chain of events leading to the present.

Each Historical Eras consists of a set of books that highlight various aspects of these major eras. For example, the Elizabethan England library features volumes on Queen Elizabeth I and her court, Elizabethan theater, the great playwrights, and everyday life in Elizabethan London.

The mini-library approach allows for the division of each era into its most significant and most interesting parts and the exploration of those parts in depth. Also, social and cultural trends as well as illustrative documents and eyewitness accounts can be prominently featured in individual volumes.

Historical Eras present a wealth of information to young readers. The lively narrative, fully documented primary and secondary source quotations, maps, photographs, sidebars, and annotated bibliographies serve as launching points for class discussion and further research.

In studying the great historical eras, students also develop a better understanding of our own times. What we learn from the past and how we apply it in the present may shape the future and may determine whether our era will be a guiding light to those traveling future roads.

Timeline

1945 Japan surrenders to Allied forces. World War II ends. U.S. General Douglas MacArthur leads Allied forces in occupation of Japan.

1947 Japan's new constitution takes effect.

1949 The Dodge Line, an economic plan created by U.S. banker Joseph Dodge, begins. The Ministry of International Trade and Industry forms to help carry out the government's plan for economic recovery.

1950 The Korean War begins.

1955 This year marks Japan's recovery from the destruction of World War II. Japan enters a period of rapid growth that continues into the 1970s. The Liberal Democratic Party forms.

1956 Japan becomes a member of the United Nations. Emperor Hirohito's son, Akihito, marries Michiko Shoda. This is the first marriage between a member of the emperor's family and a commoner.

1960 Japan and the United States renew the Treaty of Mutual Security and Cooperation. The Miike coal strike ends.

1964 Tokyo hosts the Olympic Games.

1971 U.S. president Richard M. Nixon's actions show that the friendship between Japan and the United States has weakened. The United States changes the value of the yen against the dollar, which increases the cost of Japanese goods in the United States.

1972   Japan establishes official ties with the People's Republic of China. Control of the island of Okinawa reverts from the United States to Japan.

1973   An increase in oil prices leads to a severe recession.

1981   Japanese automakers agree to limit car shipments to the United States to ease rising tensions over a trade imbalance.

1984   Toyota and General Motors open the first U.S.–Japan automobile manufacturing company in Fremont, California.

1986   Japan enacts the Equal Opportunity Employment Law.

1989   Emperor Hirohito dies. His son, Akihito, assumes the throne.

1991   The Gulf War begins. The bubble economy bursts.

1993   The Liberal Democratic Party loses control over the government for the first time since 1955.

1995   A powerful earthquake rocks Kobe, a port city in western Japan.

1997   Japan and 139 other countries sign the Kyoto Protocol, agreeing to reduce global greenhouse gases by the year 2012.

2007   Japan and the United States sign an agreement to promote nuclear power.

Introduction

After World War II

The second half of the twentieth century marked a time of dramatic change in Japan. For decades, Japan had expanded its empire and wealth through conquest. Its defeat at the end of World War II marked the end of this quest and of Japan's status as a military power. In the decades following the war, however, Japan re-emerged as a powerful global leader. It evolved from a country devastated by war to a country with one of the world's strongest economies. By the end of the twentieth century, Japan ranked among the world's wealthiest nations.

On August 15, 1945, Japanese Emperor Hirohito delivered a radio address to the nation. It was the first time in history that a Japanese emperor directly addressed his subjects. The fact that he was doing so meant something momentous was being announced. Emperor Hirohito called on his people to "endure the unendurable and suffer what is unsufferable."[1] He spoke of things not going well for Japan in the war. Although he never said that the nation had been defeated, the Japanese people knew from this broadcast that their country had lost the war.

People reacted to the emperor's announcement with a mixture of shame, relief, and grief. For years, the Japanese had believed that their armies were unstoppable, that they had fought for a good cause. Many grew up believing it was noble to "offer [oneself] courageously to the State."[2] People had delayed improvements to their communities so that money could go to the war effort. Soldiers had been encouraged to fight to the death. Civilians, too, had been asked to give their lives for their country. Surrender was not an option. After such dedication to winning the war, defeat was a bitter experience.

At the same time, many Japanese welcomed the end of the fighting. Cities lay in ruins. Factories had been destroyed, and food supplies were running low. Allied bombing had left families homeless and many children orphaned. The bombing of Tokyo on March 9, 1945, burned more than 16 square miles (41.44 sq. km) of the city. Between 80,000 and 100,000 people died in the raid. Hiroshima and Nagasaki had been leveled by atomic bombs. By the time Japan surrendered, more than 2.5 million Japanese had been killed. Millions more were injured or sick.

On September 2, 1945, Japanese officials signed the terms of surrender on the deck of the U.S. battleship *Missouri* in Tokyo Bay. Allied troops then occupied Japan for seven years. It marked the first time in Japan's history that a foreign power entered the country and took control.

During the occupation, Allied forces instituted a series of social, political, and

Emperor Hirohito and other Japanese leaders aboard the U.S.S. Missouri in 1945

Tokyo after the firebombings in 1945

such conditions, diseases spread rapidly and killed tens of thousands of people.

To rebuild the housing, hospitals, and factories that had been destroyed in the war, Japan needed resources such as lumber, metals, and stone. In the past, Japan had taken these resources from the territories it conquered. The loss of these territories created shortages of important building materials and other natural resources. In addition, Japanese shipping lines had been destroyed, so Japan could not easily import these resources from other countries.

The Japanese faced a lack of human resources as well. Millions of people had died during the war. Hundreds of thousands of soldiers never came home from prison camps in the Soviet Union. Fewer people were available to farm the land and to rebuild the country.

Numerous shortages and difficult living conditions caused exhaustion and despair in the people. As one government official described it, "we fell from heaven to hell overnight."[3] The physical and emotional devastation was so severe and widespread that it was given a name: the *kyodatsu* condition. *Kyodatsu*, coupled with rampant poverty, led to an increase in drug use and crime. Under these circumstances, the Japanese began rebuilding their country.

In spite of the many difficulties, Japan emerged twenty-five years later as one of

labor reforms (changes). Japan lost the territory that it had gained in the war. The Allies disarmed the Japanese military, and its supporters lost their jobs, were jailed, or were executed. Japanese military leaders were put on trial for war crimes. Seven of them were executed, including General Tojo Hideki, Japan's prime minister. The Allies wanted to make sure that Japan would never again wage war.

The first years after World War II were difficult for the Japanese people. They faced great emotional and physical hardships, including grief for the millions of lives lost. Widespread food shortages led to starvation. Because many homes had been destroyed, families lived in shacks or crowded together in small rooms. In

the world's wealthiest countries. Only the United States had a stronger economy. Ambitious government policies, extensive corporate freedom, and selfless devotion by workers spurred unprecedented economic growth. Japanese companies became admired for their efficiency and commitment to quality, and Japanese products became respected all over the world. Japan had achieved an economic miracle.

By the end of the twentieth century, the costs of that miracle were becoming apparent. Environmental pollution, political corruption, and a disenchanted workforce presented Japan with a new series of challenges. These challenges, which continue into the twenty-first century, give Japan yet another opportunity to reinvent itself. Whether another miracle is achieved, however, remains to be seen.

Chapter One

The Long 1950s

From 1945 to 1960, Japan worked to recover from the devastation left in the wake of World War II. Historians call this period "the long 1950s." Involvement with Western nations, especially the United States, was essential to Japan's recovery. With help from the United States, Japan evolved from a war-torn country to a wealthy nation.

The long 1950s brought fundamental changes to Japan's political structure. The emperor lost his divine status and political power when Japan became a parliamentary democracy. During this period, the Liberal Democratic Party (LDP) formed and became one of the most powerful political parties in Japan's postwar history. The LDP strongly supported economic growth in Japan and created policies that helped lead to Japan's economic success.

Japan experienced social changes as well. Concern over the U.S. military presence in Japan and U.S. nuclear testing in the Pacific led to tensions between the two countries. It also gave rise to the antinuclear movement in Japan. This movement included citizen protests against the government, a rare occurence in Japanese history.

Occupation and Recovery

The Allied powers carried out the occupation of Japan under the leadership of U.S. General Douglas MacArthur. At the signing of the surrender in September 1945, MacArthur said that "a better world shall emerge out of the blood and carnage of the past."[4] In other words, the world would recover from the destruction of World War II. MacArthur's group of mostly American Allied forces occupied Japan to help it change from a warring country led by military leaders and an emperor to a peaceful country with elected leaders.

General MacArthur supervised the American occupation of Japan after World War II.

Occupation forces had two main tasks. The first task was to take away Japan's weapons and remove all military leaders from power. The second task was to break up the concentration of wealth and power in Japan and help the nation build a peaceful democracy. These tasks would be accomplished by making reforms, or changes, in Japan's society and laws. Reforms focused on several areas, including land ownership, labor unions, business, education, and the constitution.

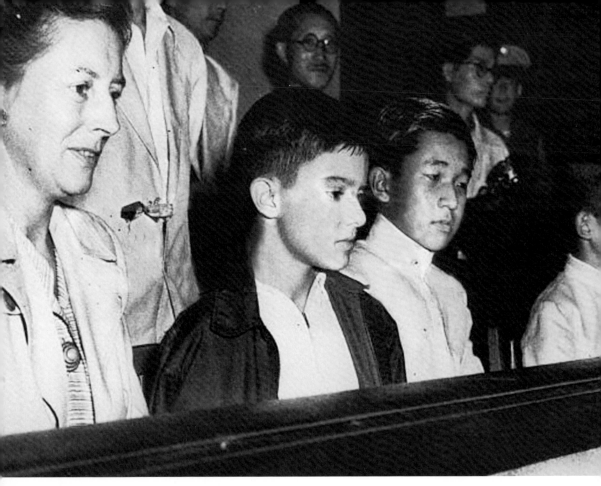

When General MacArthur became commander of the Allied occupation in Japan in 1945, he worked closely with the Emperor of Japan. Here, General MacArthur's son is seated next to the emperor's son, Crown Prince Akihito.

A New Society

The Allies wanted to improve the lives of farmers in Japan by increasing land ownership among them. Traditionally, many Japanese farmers did not own the land they farmed. They rented small tracts (pieces) of land from landowners. In 1945, farmers rented about half of Japan's farmland. The Allies changed this system. If a landowner did not live on a piece of land, the Allies divided the land into smaller tracts and distributed them to farmers. By about 1950, nearly all farmers owned most of the land they worked.

Spreading wealth in Japan meant improving the lives of workers. The Allies believed strong labor unions could help. Labor unions are groups of workers who negotiate with businesses for better pay and working conditions. When a business does not respond to such requests, union workers might go on strike. Striking workers stop doing their jobs and publicly protest the business.

Before the occupation, Japanese workers were not allowed to go on strike or ask for better pay. Business leaders made all the decisions, and workers were always expected to obey. The Allies wrote a labor law that allowed workers to form unions to argue for better conditions and to go on strike. Many Japanese liked the new law. Teachers, local government workers, factory workers, and others formed unions.

Business reform included breaking up Japan's concentration of wealth and power held by large, family-owned businesses called *zaibatsu*. They controlled many banks, factories, shipping companies and trading companies, which import and export goods. At first, the Allies split many of these companies into smaller ones. By the end of the occupation, however, the Allies had decided that these large businesses could help Japan rebuild, so they allowed the zaibatsu to continue.

Educational reforms included revising school textbooks. Japanese textbooks had been a government tool used to influence

To encourage a less militaristic society following the war, the Allies enacted educational reforms and taught Japanese students about democracy.

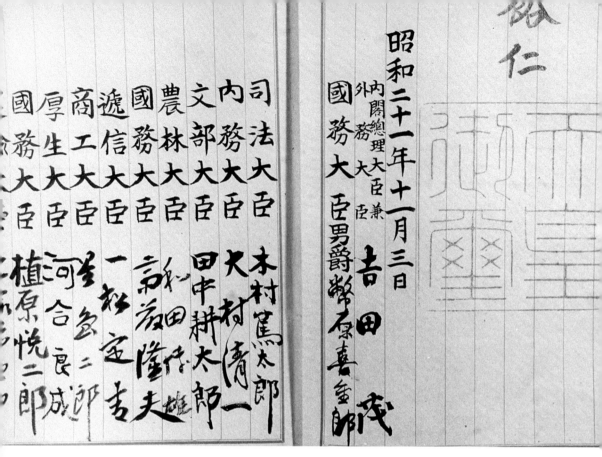

The new constitution came into effect in Japan in 1947. Emperor Hirohito's signature (top right) and seal (bottom right) are seen on the original document.

people. They stated that the Japanese were a superior people and that it was important to support the military and its wars aimed at conquering other countries. The Allies removed this propaganda. They believed it was important to remove these old ideas from the schoolbooks so that Japanese children could learn how to live in a democracy. The Allies encouraged new teaching methods that promoted independent thinking and changed the number of years children should attend school from six years to nine years.

The New Constitution

Perhaps the most important change in Japan after World War II was the creation of a new constitution. A constitution describes the basic laws of a nation. The Allies wanted to change the laws of Japan to create a democracy and to destroy the ruling powers of the aristocracy and the military.

The new constitution of Japan took effect in 1947 and brought about great changes in Japan's society and laws. It eliminated the military and the ruling power of the emperor, who became merely a symbol of Japan. The constitution set up a British-style parliamentary system of government. Under this system, the legislature, called the Diet, became Japan's top lawmaking group. The head of the government became the prime minister, who was chosen by members of the Diet.

Civil rights expanded under the constitution. Women received the right to vote. Girls were given the same right as boys to inherit family property. Freedom of speech increased, and people were allowed to criticize the government. To protect these rights, the new constitution established an independent system of judges.

Facing Shortages

The people of Japan put their energy into the huge task of rebuilding the country. They needed energy sources such as coal, building materials such as lumber and steel, and many other resources for daily life, such as rubber, textiles, and paper. In the past, Japan had gotten resources and materials from the countries it conquered, but it had lost those territories and resources. What few resources were left in Japan were often only available at very high prices. These conditions made it difficult for the Japanese to start rebuilding.

In 1949, Japanese students in Tokyo celebrated May Day, an international worker's holiday. Their signs call for peace and independence.

Food Shortages

Finding food became a priority for many Japanese after the war. Some city dwellers went to the countryside to bargain with farmers. Many traded clothing, jewelry, and other prized possessions for

food. Even children focused on helping the family get food. An article titled "Let's Catch Grasshoppers" in one girls' magazine discussed eating grasshoppers as a source of protein. To help prevent massive starvation, the United States began shipping food to Japan in 1945, but shortages continued. In May 1946, about 250,000 women and children gathered in front of the emperor's palace, demanding food. They knew that the emperor was not suffering as they were. This protest became known as Food May Day. The emperor expressed concern over the people's suffering, but he seemed unable to do more. The United States increased food shipments, which helped the Japanese survive.

Food shortages in 1946 forced children to scavenge for any food they could find.

The Government's Plan for Recovery

With the support of the United States, the Japanese government began to guide rebuilding efforts. The recovery plan focused on giving the most help to industries that were likely to grow, including steel, chemical, and shipbuilding companies and energy producers, such as coal and electric power companies. Government leaders made sure that these industries got the money, raw materials, machinery, and workers they needed.

These industries also received tax cuts. Taxes are money that businesses and people must give to the government to pay for things such as roads, schools, and parks. A tax cut reduces the amount of taxes that must be paid. Tax cuts for industries in Japan left more money for buying machinery, paying workers, and other costs associated with business.

The Dodge Line

By the late 1940s, Japan was still struggling, and U.S. leaders decided that Japan needed more help. They hired Joseph Dodge, a banker, to create an economic plan for Japan. The plan, called the Dodge Line, began in 1949 and included making Japanese goods inexpensive to buyers in other countries. Dodge thought that if Japanese products were cheap, people around the world would buy them. More sales would help Japanese businesses succeed.

The Dodge Line forced the government to cut its spending. Japanese leaders cut the amount of money they funneled to their favorite industries as well as money for schools, health care, and public works. With less money coming in, business leaders had to cut jobs. Unemployed people then had less money to spend on goods. With fewer people spending money, more businesses began to fail. In addition, cheap Japanese goods did not sell to other countries as well as expected. By 1950, Japan seemed to be headed for an economic depression. Then, in June 1950, the Korean War broke out and changed everything.

The Korean War

United Nations troops from sixteen countries fought communist forces from North Korea and China in the Korean War. The war became one of the bloodiest wars in history. During the war, the United States bought equipment for United Nations forces and relied on Japan to produce much of it. Steel, machines, clothing, chemicals, lumber, paper, and automobiles were among the many products that Japanese industries sold to the United States.

The demand for products increased profits in Japan and saved some companies from failure, including the carmaker Toyota. Toyota's president said that car orders during the Korean War were "Toyota's salvation."[5] The economic boom helped industries survive a difficult time and led to greater prosperity for many Japanese people. Nonetheless, some Japanese people felt misgivings about profiting from a war. Toyota's president said, "I felt a mingling of joy for my company and a sense of guilt that I was rejoicing over another country's war."[6]

The Turning Point

The year 1955 marked a turning point for Japan. That year, Japan officially recovered from the destruction of World War II. U.S. support in the form of food, materials, money loans, and military defense was key to Japan's recovery. A large part of Japan's recovery also came from equipment sales to the United States during the Korean War. The Japanese did their share, however, through the actions of experienced business managers, people working hard and saving their money, and continued government guidance.

The demand for products during the Korean War helped Japanese-owned Toyota become a powerful automaker. In the 1950s, Toyota began exporting cars to the United States.

The Importance of Experience, Work, and Savings

Japan benefited from its experience as an industrial nation. Unlike countries trying to start industries such as auto manufacturing and steel plants for the first time, Japan had built such industries before. It had experienced managers who knew how to build and run businesses.

In addition, Japan had a ready supply of motivated workers. The war had destroyed many factories, which left about ten million people without jobs. They wanted to work hard to rebuild their country.

The Japanese ethic of saving money helped the economy. Though much of the country had been destroyed, the Japanese were still able to save some of their money. Older people with memories of the war put money in savings accounts to help protect themselves from an uncertain future. Younger people saved for education, health care, consumer goods, and retirement. Banks turned these savings into loans for businesses, which fueled economic growth.

Most government guidance came from a group called the Ministry of International Trade and Industry (MITI). The group formed in 1949 to help carry out the government's recovery plan. One important role of MITI was to buy advanced technology from the United States and give it to businesses that the Japanese government wanted to support.

The LDP

In 1955, two political parties, the Liberals and the Democrats, joined to make

Following the war, many Japanese were eager to work. This workforce helped spur Japan's economy. Many people went to work in the expanding steel industry.

one party, the Liberal Democratic Party (LDP). By making economic growth its top priority, the LDP continued to guide the rebuilding of the country and its industries.

The LDP encouraged growth of factories on the Pacific coast near shipping centers. It built and improved major roads, railways, and ports so businesses could easily transport goods across Japan and to other countries. The party also encouraged cities, towns, and rural areas to attract industries. Factories meant jobs and more income, so areas competed with each other to get these businesses, offering such gifts as tax cuts and land for the factories.

Following the United States

The United States feared the spread of communism in Asia in the decades following World War II. As a result, it encouraged Japan to avoid doing business with its two large communist neighbors, the Soviet Union and China.

Japan already had some difficulties with the Soviets. The nation was bitter over the loss of thousands of Japanese soldiers who had never returned from Siberian prison camps after the war. Both

The *Keiretsu*

When Japan industrialized in the late 1800s, large family-owned businesses known as zaibatsu dictated the economy. Zaibatsu included companies such as Mitsubishi, Mitsui, and Sumitomo. Mitsubishi started as a shipping company. Mitsui had been producing silk since the seventeenth century, and Sumitomo had been Japan's chief copper-mining company. The 1950s saw the development of a system similar to the zaibatsu, but instead of industrial and manufacturing companies, the companies were commercial, or bank based. These commercial giants were called *keiretsu*.

Mitsubishi, Mitsui, and Sumitomo reconfigured themselves to become keiretsu. New keiretsu formed, including Fuji and Sanwa. Unlike the zaibatsu, the keiretsu were not family controlled. They were more willing to deal with outsiders and to hire based on ability rather than family name. Such policies made the keiretsu much more flexible and able to respond to global and technological changes than the zaibatsu had been.

At first, some saw keiretsu as abnormal and un-Japanese. That view changed as the keiretsu proved their ability to adapt to and prosper in the global economy.

countries also claimed ownership of certain islands in the region, and the ownership was not yet settled.

Japan did not have difficulties with China. Japanese leaders viewed China's population as a huge group of potential customers, but they did not want to risk making the United States angry by trading with its communist neighbor. As a result, Japan looked for interested customers elsewhere and forced thousands of suspected communists from their jobs to prevent the growth of the Communist Party in Japan.

Because Japan helped discourage the growth of communism in Asia, the United States supported its membership in the United Nations (UN), a large organization that works for world peace, security, and human rights. Japanese leaders believed membership in the UN was crucial to becoming a respected, independent nation in the world. In 1956, through the support of the United States and the work of the LDP, Japan became a member of the UN.

Growing Opposition

As Japan became stronger, some members of the LDP resented certain changes the United States had forced on them. In particular, they wanted to drop Article 9 of the constitution. This article eliminated the military and stated that Japan must never make war or have weapons of war again. Some felt that this reform left Japan defenseless. They argued that independent countries have a right to defend themselves. Not enough Japanese lawmakers supported the idea to change the constitution, but the complaints became part of growing opposition to the United States.

By the 1950s, the Japanese had mixed feelings about the influence of the United States in Japan and the world. At the end of World War II, U.S. soldiers and products flooded into Japan. At first, the Japanese appreciated the food, financial aid, and other support. The soldiers gave gum and chocolate to children, who were said to have quickly learned "give me chocolate" as one of their first English phrases.

After a few years, however, the Japanese began to resent the soldiers. This was partly due to a growing desire for full independence from the United States and partly due to actions of the U.S. military. For example, the United States had used Japan as a military base of operations during the Korean War. Many Japanese had misgivings about this connection to another country's war.

The U.S. military had expanded its airplane runways in Japan to allow larger planes to land during the Korean War. Japan is a small country with less land area than California, and much of that land is covered with mountains. The Japanese already felt squeezed by the small amount of land available to meet

In the 1950s, U.S. products flooded Japan. As a result of American soldiers passing out candy, many Japanese children learned "give me chocolate" as their first English words.

increasing demands for factories, farms, and homes. In addition, some U.S. military personnel committed crimes during the occupation, which added to growing resentment.

The Antinuclear Movement

Memories of the devastation caused by the atomic bombs dropped on Hiroshima and Nagasaki added to resentment against the United States. The Japanese held memorials every year on August 6, the anniversary of the bombing of Hiroshima. These gatherings became part of a growing antinuclear movement.

The antinuclear movement gained strength after the United States tested a

The Memorial Monument for Hiroshima was built in 1952. The stone chest in the center holds a list of the names of all the people who died in the nuclear bombing.

nuclear bomb over the Pacific Ocean in 1954. Hundreds of people on islands in the Pacific became sick from the fallout of the test. Fallout is radioactive material that settles to the earth after a nuclear explosion. Exposure to fallout can make people sick. Reaction to the incident triggered greater Japanese opposition to the United States. Annual memorials at Hiroshima grew into large protests against U.S. nuclear testing.

The 1960 Security Treaty

Increased tensions between the United States and Japan led the countries to consider changing the 1951 security treaty. This treaty allowed the United States to indefinitely use Japan as a military base for "the maintenance of international

The *Lucky Dragon* Incident

At the time of the nuclear test, a Japanese fishing vessel called the Lucky Dragon was on the ocean. The boat's crew witnessed a blast that was about one thousand times more powerful than the bomb dropped on Hiroshima. One crew member said that "the sky in the west suddenly lit up and the sea became brighter than day."[1] He recalled watching the event with his crewmates: "We watched the dazzling light, which felt heavy. Seven or eight minutes later there was a terrific sound—like an avalanche. Then a visible multi-colored ball of fire appeared on the horizon."[2]

Hours after the blast, white ash fell on the Lucky Dragon. This ash was part of the nuclear fallout from the blast. Everyone on the fishing boat became sick by the end of the day, and one crew member eventually died from exposure to radiation.

[1]Bruce Kennedy, "The Lucky Dragon," CNN.com, http://www.cnn.com/SPECIALS/cold.war/episodes/08/spotlight/(accessed March 22, 2007).

[2]Ibid.

peace and security in the Far East" and the "security of Japan."[7] U.S. soldiers could act as a police force in Japan. Many Japanese thought these rules gave a foreign power too much control in their country.

In 1960, the countries changed the treaty. The new treaty stated that the United States needed permission from Japan to use its Japanese bases to fight wars in Asia and to bring nuclear weapons to Japan. When leaders quickly approved these changes, massive protests broke out. Many Japanese thought that the government had not listened to their concerns about the treaty. Hundreds of thousands of people, including students, workers, and housewives, gathered on the streets of Tokyo and around the parliament building in protest. The demonstrators failed to prevent approval of the treaty, but their actions showed that the Japanese people were willing to stand up and express their opposition to a government policy.

U.S. President Dwight D. Eisenhower cancelled a state visit to Japan because the protests against the 1960 Security Treaty were so large.

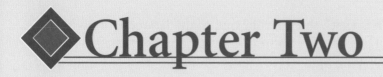

Chapter Two

Double-Digit Growth: The 1960s

Japan experienced rapid economic growth during the 1960s. A dramatic increase in business led to more jobs and greater prosperity. Some people called this growth an economic miracle because it happened so fast. Japan went from being a country devastated by war to being an industrial power.

The rapid industrial growth of the 1960s came at a cost. Cities became crowded as people moved there for jobs. The environment became polluted. Protest groups formed to take action against pollution and other problems in Japan. These groups tried to change laws and business practices to improve people's lives.

The Shift to Oil

Economic growth was the government's top priority in the 1960s. The government supported increased industrial production, shipbuilding, and chemical manufacturing. These industries required large amounts of energy.

Coal was the main source of energy for Japanese industries. In 1950, coal supplied 60 percent of the country's energy needs. Oil supplied about 7 percent. Much of Japan's coal came from mines in Kyushu.

In the 1950s, business and political leaders shifted from coal to oil as the main industrial energy source. Oil from the Middle East had become a cheaper energy source than Japanese coal. By 1970, oil supplied more than 70 percent of Japan's energy needs.

The Japanese built factories, oil refineries, and power stations by the sea. The new facilities were closer to the tankers that brought oil from the Middle East. The refineries processed the oil and sent it to power stations. Power stations then supplied factories with the energy they needed.

Japan's industry boom in the 1960s created more demand for energy sources, such as oil.

The decision to shift to oil was controversial. It made Japan dependent on foreign energy sources. Some people argued that it was unwise to rely on other countries. Coal companies and miners complained about the business lost to the oil industry.

Managers of coal companies were forced to reduce expenses. Many workers lost their jobs. In 1959, the Mitsui Mining and Smelting Company cut 1,200 workers from the mines in Kyushu. The miners organized a strike to protest the cutbacks.

The Strike at Miike Mines

The strike lasted about nine months. Hundreds of thousands of people became involved. At one point, almost 10,000 police showed up to confront the strikers. Workers protested the lost jobs as well as the change from coal to oil. Many workers did not want Japan to help big businesses to profit through a cheap foreign energy source, because those profits caused job cuts in energy-related Japanese industries, such as coal mining.

The strike was harder on the miners than on the mining company, which refused to pay the strikers. Labor unions raised money to give to these workers. The money from the unions helped, but it was only about a third of a miner's usual pay. On the other hand, the mining company had support from banks and government leaders. For example, the company was able to sell coal from other mines. With this support, the company stayed in business and refused to meet the strikers' demands.

The strike ended on November 1, 1960, after the government helped settle the dispute. The government did not force the mine to rehire all the workers. It did, however, help bring higher wages and better working conditions for

In 1960, workers at the Mitsui Miike mine went on strike to protest job cutbacks that were caused by lost business to overseas oil companies.

miners. The strike remains the longest strike in Japan's postwar history.

Government leaders and labor union leaders learned from the strike. Government leaders learned that social unrest can result from decisions that cause unemployment. They realized that they needed to help people get new jobs, so they set up programs to train unemployed workers in new fields. In addition, government leaders offered housing to encourage unemployed people to move to new jobs. Labor union leaders learned that long strikes are not always effective. They decided that negotiating for better wages would be more productive than striking.

The coal industry continued to cut jobs. In 1960, about 300,000 people worked in coal mines. By the early 1970s, only about 40,000 people worked in mines.

Ikeda Hayato was Japan's prime minister from 1960 to 1964. He was instrumental in Japan's economic growth.

More Civil Unrest

The miners' strike came at a time of social unrest in Japan. Many people, including students, held protests against Japan's security treaty with the United States. This treaty allowed the United States to continue operating military bases in Japan. Opposition to the bases had been building through the 1950s. Many Japanese believed that the presence of U.S. troops kept Japan under the control of the United States.

To quiet the unrest, the leader of the government, Prime Minister Ikeda Hayato, laid out a plan. He wanted the Japanese to focus on building a stronger economy and greater prosperity. Ikeda's plan, announced in 1960, was called the Income Doubling Plan.

Rapid Growth

Ikeda designed the Income Doubling Plan to double people's average income in ten years. In addition, he wanted to double the nation's gross national product (GNP) in ten years. The GNP is the value of all the goods and services that a nation produces in one year.

Most Japanese people liked the plan. Their lives had improved in the years after World War II, but they were eager for greater prosperity.

The Goals of the Income Doubling Plan

The Income Doubling Plan had several goals. One goal was to increase the number of consumer products. Another goal was to make quality machinery and other high-priced items that were in demand around the world. Ikeda hoped that these goals would rid Japan of low-wage jobs and boost employment.

The Income Doubling Plan required a large increase in imports and exports. Imports are goods and raw materials that are shipped into a country. Exports are products and raw materials that are shipped out of a country. In the past, because Japan had few natural resources, the country had imported more than it exported. After several years of rapid growth in Japan's industries, however, exports outstripped imports. Japan still imported huge amounts of fuel to power its growing industries. By the early 1970s, more than 80 percent of these energy resources came from outside the country. The largest energy resource was oil from the Middle East.

The Economic Miracle

Tremendous economic growth continued in Japan throughout the 1960s and into the 1970s. Each year, Japan's economic growth averaged at least 10 percent. In other words, the value of all Japan's products and services was worth 10 percent more each year. In comparison, the U.S. economy grew at less than 5 percent per year. The economy of the United Kingdom averaged only about 3 percent growth per year.

The growth came from increases in the quality and quantity of products made in Japan, particularly from the chemical, electronic, and machine-building industries. Production of high-quality consumer goods, such as televisions and electrical appliances, increased. Sales of cars, cameras, and audio and video equipment grew rapidly.

The Japanese government, business leaders, and workers all contributed to economic growth. Government leaders continued some practices from the 1950s. They supported bank loans to chemical, steel, shipbuilding, and oil-refining companies. The government also funneled advanced technology to industries that could profit most from it. Support for the construction of roads, bridges, railways, and ports continued. Business leaders poured money into new factories and equipment. Workers stayed long hours in offices and factories, and most of them worked six days each week. People continued to save money. By the end of the 1960s, most Japanese saved about 25 percent of their available money.

Higher Wages Lead to More Consumer Spending

Factories, plants, and other businesses sprang up or expanded quickly. Japan had more jobs available than it had workers to fill them. Wages rose because companies

Japan's strong economy throughout the 1960s and 1970s led to a demand in consumer products, such as electronics.

had to offer good pay to keep their employees happy. Otherwise, the employees would leave and find other jobs.

With the increase in income, people had more money to spend. Electric appliances, such as rice cookers and stoves, were especially popular with Japanese consumers. Many people began to fill their homes with modern products such as televisions and washing machines. Higher sales of consumer goods fueled economic growth. In fact, most items that Japanese companies made in the 1960s were purchased by the Japanese people themselves.

The Income Doubling Plan Succeeds

The Income Doubling Plan succeeded well before the end of the 1960s, due to tremendous growth in the production of goods and the large increase in consumer spending. By 1968, Japan had achieved Ikeda-

The Wage Gap Between Men and Women in the 1960s

Traditionally, the Japanese government's position was that women should take care of the household and children. The phrase "good wife, wise mother" described this role.[1]

In the 1950s and 1960s, government leaders began to encourage women to take part in Japan's growing industrial economy. At the same time, however, women were expected to give up full-time work when they married or gave birth. Sometimes, women returned to work part-time after their children were grown. These women were paid less than men. Companies paid and promoted workers based on how long they had worked full-time at the company. As a result, wages for women did not improve at the same rate as they did for men during the 1960s.

[1] Andrew Gordon, *Postwar Japan as History* (Berkeley: University of California, 1993), 294.

Hayato's goal of doubling the national income. That year, most Western standards ranked Japan as the world's second-largest economy. The only country with a larger economy was the United States.

The Costs of Rapid Growth

The rapid growth of industrial areas along the Pacific coast boosted Japan's wealth, but this prosperity came with certain costs. Prime Minister Tanaka Kakeui spoke about some of these costs in 1972:

> The rapid economic growth of postwar Japan, particularly since the mid-1950s, has spurred industrialization and urbanization throughout the nation. The result has been the excessive concentration of both population and industry in the Tokyo-Nagoya-Osaka belt along the Pacific coast, forming a hyper-dense community the likes of which is not to be found elsewhere in the world. All of the major industrial nations of the world are today faced with the common agonies of inflation, urban deterioration, environmental pollution, stagnant agriculture, and spiritual frustration amidst material affluence. This is especially so in Japan. Smaller than the single state of California, Japan has nearly one-third of the people concentrated on a mere one percent of the land, making the tempo of social and economic change so much the greater.[8]

The Tokyo Olympics

Tokyo served as the site of the Summer Olympics in 1964. The Japanese took great pride in hosting the games. The prime minister of Japan described the 1964 games as a chance for the world to "engage in peaceful competition" and to see how Japan had grown into a peaceful society.[1] To symbolize how far Japan had come since World War II, Yoshinori Sakai lit the Olympic flame at the opening ceremonies. Yoshinori was the first child born in Hiroshima on the day the atomic bomb was dropped on that city.

The Olympics spurred construction of subways, hotels, and sports centers. The government built a high-speed railway line called the *Tokaido Shinkansen*, or bullet train. Existing roadways, subways, sewer systems, and water systems were improved.

The Tokyo Olympics marked the first time the Olympics were held in Asia. In addition, judo and volleyball became Olympic events for the first time that year.

[1]Andrew Gordon, *Postwar Japan as History* (Berkeley: University of California, 1993), 72.

Japan used the 1964 Tokyo Summer Olympics as a way to show the world how it had become a peaceful nation since World War II.

Japan had experienced great social changes along with its economic growth. As a result, the Japanese people faced some major problems. Two of the most serious problems were crowded living conditions and environmental pollution.

Population Growth in Cities

People increasingly moved to cities for jobs during the 1960s. At the start of the decade, about two-thirds of all Japanese lived in cities. Fifteen years later, about three-fourths of all Japanese lived in cities. Tokyo's population topped eight million, making it the world's largest city. High-

Beginning in the 1960s, many Japanese began moving into cities, such as Tokyo, in pursuit of work. This created problems with overcrowding and pollution.

rise buildings filled city skylines. As urban populations grew and space became tight, the cost of land rose. Prices went so high that middle-class people could not afford to buy homes. Most people had to live in small houses or apartments.

Rapid population growth in the cities led to traffic congestion as streets became crowded with cars. Travel time to and from work increased. Commuter railways became so full that attendants had to shove people into the trains so that the doors could close.

Environmental Pollution and Citizens' Movements

Industries and urban congestion along the Pacific coast affected Japan's environment. Without laws to prevent companies from polluting the air or dumping waste into rivers, the environment's quality rapidly declined. Chemicals flowed into rivers and created foamy scum along ocean shores. These chemicals polluted the water and killed fish populations. Smog filled the sky. Mount Fuji could not be seen from Tokyo for most of the year. In some places, the air was so polluted that the government set up oxygen stations for people. Japan had become one of the most polluted countries in the world.

Many people developed illnesses from pollution of the air and water. One example occurred near Minamata on the west side of the Japanese island of Kyushu.

Minamata Disease

In the 1950s, people in Minamata noticed dead fish floating in Minamata Bay. The area's cats began to wobble and stumble around. People called this behavior "cat dancing," but it was clear that something was wrong with the animals.

People in the area soon began to suffer from physical and mental disorders. Some had trouble walking. Others had numbness in their hands so they could not write or button shirts. Some people died. Babies born in the area had brain damage.

Doctors called the sickness Minamata disease. They believed the people were being poisoned. Experts then determined what the sick people and cats had in common: They had eaten fish from the bay. These fish had been poisoned by mercury from the Chisso Corporation, which had an industrial plant in Minamata. The plant made a chemical fertilizer. Mercury was one of the waste products of the plant's industrial processes. Chisso dumped its waste into Minamata Bay, and the mercury poisoned the fish. When people and cats ate the fish, they were poisoned, too.

Public Response to Pollution Problems

For years, Chisso officials refused to admit that the plant was responsible for causing people's health problems. Finally, people sued the company and won in court. The company had to pay the victims. In 1968, the Japanese government banned the Chisso Corporation from putting mercury into the waters of Minamata Bay.

Protests concerning the tragic consequences of pollution around Minamata and other areas were part of a growing antipollution movement in the late 1960s. People urged the Japanese government to take action against polluters. In 1970, the lawmaking branch of the government, known as the Diet, passed many laws to protect the environment. As a result, this session of the Diet became known as the Pollution Diet.

Citizen Protests

Citizen groups gathered to protest sever-

It hurts! It hurts!

For many years, people near the Jinzu River in central Japan showed symptoms of a rare illness. The illness was so painful that people cried out, "*Itai! Itai!*" when touched. The word *itai* means "It hurts." In the most severe cases of the illness, a person could not even move without breaking a bone. People named the disease itai-itai.

In 1968, the Japanese government found that the metal cadmium caused itai-itai. In the body, cadmium causes kidney damage and calcium deficiency. Without calcium, bones become brittle and can easily break. The government found cadmium in the Jinzu River. Experts traced the cadmium to pollution that entered the waterways from a mine belonging to the Mitsui Mining and Smelting Company.

Victims tried to convince the company to take responsibility and fix the problem. Instead, the company blamed the disease on health issues, such as poor diet and sanitation. Victims of the poisoning sued the company and won. This lawsuit and others raised awareness in Japan of the importance of protecting the environment and people's health.

al different issues in the 1960s. They protested the spread of industry into certain agricultural areas, the construction of a Tokyo airport on farmland, and the increasing number of high-rise buildings that blocked sunshine. Many groups also protested U.S. influence in Japan.

Rising Tensions with the United States

Tensions between Japan and the United States had been rising since the 1950s. Many people protested the 1960 security treaty that allowed the U.S. military to keep bases in Japan. Some Japanese objected to the U.S. military's control and use of the Japanese island of Okinawa. Others opposed Japan's participation in the Vietnam War.

Communist Vietnamese fought noncommunist Vietnamese in the Vietnam War. During the 1950s, Vietnam was divided into North Vietnam, which was communist, and South Vietnam, which was not. The United States joined the South Vietnamese to try to prevent the North Vietnamese from taking over all of Vietnam.

U.S. military bases in Japan were important to the United States during the war. With Japan's permission, the United States used its naval bases to restock nuclear submarines. In addition, Japanese industries made supplies that U.S. forces used in the war.

The Antiwar Movement

Some Japanese became uncomfortable with the U.S. involvement in Vietnam. They believed that the United States should not interfere in the problems of other countries. Some also worried that the war could spread to Japan. Protests against the war began in 1965, and millions of people became involved. One of the largest protests took place in 1968 after a nuclear-powered U.S. aircraft carrier arrived near Nagasaki.

Soon after the aircraft carrier left, Japan took a strong stance against nuclear weapons. Prime Minister Sato Eisaku later announced the nation's Three Non-Nuclear Principles. These principles stated that Japan would not make nuclear weapons, own nuclear weapons, or allow nuclear weapons into the country. Sato won the 1974 Nobel Peace Prize for his efforts to pursue Japan's goals by peaceful means.

Conclusion

Economic growth brought prosperity to many people in Japan in the 1960s. This growth led to changes in the Japanese lifestyle and caused environmental pollution in cities and industrial areas. The Japanese people began to challenge certain government and business priorities. Citizen groups and labor unions protested social and health problems that resulted from Japan's rapid economic growth. Some people opposed U.S. activities in Asia. The Japanese government continued to support economic growth during the 1960s and took steps to address the resulting social and environmental problems.

Sato Eisaku was prime minister of Japan from 1964 to 1972.

Chapter Three

Shocked! The 1970s

By the end of the 1960s, the Japanese had experienced more than a decade of rising wealth. This wealth had been built with support from the United States, affordable resources, and hard work. In the 1970s, however, international events weakened Japanese trust in the United States. Japan also lost the supply of cheap energy that had fueled its economy.

An oil crisis in the 1970s thrust Japan into its worst recession since World War II. The nation recovered quickly but people were shaken. Economic uncertainty and tensions with the United States led to protests against the United States. Because of these challenges and a public corruption scandal, the leading Japanese political party, the Liberal Democratic Party (LDP), lost support. Meanwhile, the U.S. government and many U.S. businesses took action to stop the rising sales of Japanese products in the United States.

Problems with the U. S.

During the 1960s, many Japanese found their voice in protesting a variety of causes, such as the 1960 security treaty with the United States and the layoffs at the Miike mines. Such protests of the 1960s spilled into the 1970s. Some of these protests were about control of Okinawa, a small island south of Japan. The Japanese had controlled Okinawa before World War II. In 1945, U.S. forces had fought the Japanese there.

After the war, the United States took control of the island, which became a base for nuclear-powered submarines as well as a storage place for nuclear weapons. U.S. military forces used Okinawa during the Korean War in the 1950s and the Vietnam War in the 1960s.

The people of Okinawa resented U.S. control of the island. Along with other Japanese, they demanded its return to Japanese control. In 1972, Okinawa was

In the 1970s, the American military presence on Okinawa created tensions between the United States and Japan.

returned to Japan. The United States was allowed to keep its military bases on the island but could no longer store nuclear weapons there.

Doing Business with China

The attitude of U.S. leaders toward China frustrated most Japanese, who viewed China as a natural business partner. China was nearby and had a huge number of potential customers. Japan, however, had to follow U.S. policy on China. As a result, Japan limited its business with China.

After World War II, the Communist Party in China fought a war against the Chinese Nationalist Party. In 1949, the Nationalists lost the war and fled to the island of Taiwan. The Communists then established the People's Republic of China (PRC) on the Chinese mainland. The Nationalists established the Republic of China (ROC) on Taiwan. Both groups remained bitter enemies.

U.S. leaders wanted to discourage other countries from doing business with mainland China. They believed that business deals could strengthen China and lead to the spread of communist ideas. Because of Japan's interest in China, however, U.S. leaders promised to tell Japanese leaders about any changes in policy.

Officially, Japan limited business with China. Even so, by 1970, Japan had become China's main business partner.

Nixon's Irritation with Japan

U.S. President Richard M. Nixon had grown irritated with the Japanese by the early 1970s. At the time, the United States still carried the responsibility and cost of defending Japan. Nixon believed that the Japanese should take on more of their defense costs. He thought that his promise to return Okinawa ensured that Japanese leaders would do him a favor. Nixon wanted the Japanese to reduce shipments of inexpensive textiles to the Unit-

By opening trade with China in 1971, Japan felt that President Nixon had betrayed them.

ed States, which would make U.S. textile makers happy. When Japanese leaders failed to take immediate action, Nixon opened ties to China without telling Japan.

The Nixon Shocks

In July 1971, U.S. leaders announced that they had been secretly talking with mainland China. President Nixon visited China in 1972. The announcement, and visit, were two of several actions that the Japanese called the Nixon shocks. A Japanese government official later described these U.S. actions as a betrayal: "There was resentment over the fact that the United States had gone ahead of Japan in opening up contact with China."[9]

Japan felt it had special ties with China that dated back into ancient history. At the request of the United States, Japan had not acted on those feelings of kinship and did not open China as a business market during the years of economic growth in the 1960s. When the Nixon administration and the United States agreed to begin trading with China, Japanese leaders saw it as a slap in the face.

Another shock was the cost of goods shipped to the United States from Japan. U.S. leaders added a fee on all imports coming into the United States. This fee raised the price of Japanese goods by 10 percent. Unemployment was growing in the United States. Nixon wanted Americans to buy more U.S. goods. He believed that increased demand for U.S. goods would boost production and create more jobs. At the same time, however, Japanese businesses suffered from a loss of U.S. customers.

One more shock was the new exchange rate between the Japanese currency, called the yen, and the U.S. dollar. This rate had been set in the 1940s. It described how many yen were worth one dollar. The old rate ensured that the cost of Japanese goods was cheap for U.S. buyers. When the United States changed the rate, the cost of Japanese goods went up. For example, in 1949, 360 yen equaled 1 dollar. In 1973, 230 yen equaled 1 dollar. The change meant that a Japanese item that cost 50 dollars in 1971 cost 78 dollars by 1973.

The new exchange rate led Japanese businesses to change some of their policies. Because the yen was worth more, Japanese businesses could buy more materials with it. Some businesses cut their prices because their costs were lower. These cuts lowered the price of Japanese goods around the world. Demand for Japanese goods rose once again.

Reaction to the Shocks

The Nixon shocks hurt Japanese pride. The Japanese reacted by increasing their business ties with China. In 1972, Japanese leaders set up an agreement with China. It ended hostility that remained from previous wars and expanded business between the two countries. Six years later, in August 1978, Japanese and Chinese leaders officially signed a Treaty

Asakai's Nightmare

In the late 1950s, a Japanese ambassador to the United States, Asakai Koichiro, had a dream. He dreamed that the United States suddenly changed its policy toward China without telling Japan. The story became known as Asakai's Nightmare.

U.S. government officials called Japan's ambassador shortly before Nixon announced the sudden change in policy toward China in 1971. The shocked ambassador cried out "the Asakai nightmare has happened."[1] Minutes later, Prime Minister Sato Eisaku learned about the announcement. The change surprised and embarrassed the Japanese. They wondered whether U.S. friendship was sincere.

This event fueled frustration with the United States. At the same time, however, there was a growing sense of national pride among the Japanese. They had achieved great success in business. Many were tired of U.S. control over their affairs.

[1]Quoted in Michael Schaller, "The Nixon 'Shocks' and U.S.-Japan Strategic Relations, 1964–74," (Working Paper No. 5, The National Security Archive, US-Japan Special Documentation Project, 1996), http://www.gwu.edu/~nsarchiv/japan/soeya.htm (accessed April 8, 2007).

Nixon's visit to China in 1972 marked the first time a U.S. president had visited communist China.

of Peace and Friendship.

The shocks made the Japanese aware of how vulnerable they were to outside forces. Some people were concerned about Japan's dependence on foreign oil. The Japanese used oil for heat and electricity. Oil powered the nation's industries. About three-fourths of Japan's energy came from oil sources outside Japan. Most of this oil came from the Middle East.

Japan's wealth was built upon a delicate balance of access to cheap resources, U.S. support, and the hard work of the Japanese people. Nixon's shocks made many Japanese unsure of their country's relationship with the United States. A global oil crisis then brought Japan's rapid growth to an abrupt halt.

The End of Rapid Economic Growth

In 1973, the Organization of Petroleum Exporting Countries (OPEC) quadrupled the price of oil. The price increase affected countries around the world. In Japan, it meant the end of rapid economic growth.

Japanese people worried about the oil price increase. Many still remembered the economic struggles after World War II. Fearing a repeat of that experience, they began to stock up on supplies. Businesses kept goods that they made. This led to shortages in some consumer products.

The increase in oil prices hit large businesses hard. Steel plants, shipbuilding companies, and chemical companies had to spend more money to make their products.

The Japanese government ordered cuts in the use of oil. Less oil forced factories and industries to produce fewer goods. As a result, shortages caused prices to rise. Prices rose by about 30 percent from 1973 to 1974.

The rise in oil prices led to the worst recession in Japan since the end of World War II. A recession is a decrease in the amount of business activity in a country. There is less buying, selling, and producing of goods. This economic slowdown can result in job cuts.

Surviving the Recession

Companies used several methods to survive the recession. They cut energy use and reduced production. Some factories used more machines and fewer people to assemble parts. Due to the system of lifetime employment, however, most businesses avoided cutting workers. Instead, they awarded fewer promotions, encouraged older workers to retire, and hired part-time or temporary workers. Many women took these part-time jobs. Some part-time jobs involved the same work as permanent jobs, but they paid less.

Government leaders also shifted support away from industries that depended on large amounts of energy and imported raw materials. Instead, they focused on knowledge industries, which are businesses that grow through technological innovation. These businesses did not rely on a huge supply of energy or imported materials. Electronics became an important knowledge industry in Japan. This industry offered many opportunities for innovation. Japanese businesses succeeded in developing high-quality videotape recorders, computers, and other electronic items.

Automobile manufacturing was another knowledge industry. In the 1970s,

Japanese carmakers responded to the oil crisis by producing cars that used less gasoline. Their focus on energy efficiency paid off. By the end of the decade, Japan produced more cars than the United States.

After oil prices increased again in 1979, the Japanese government began a program of energy conservation. Government and business leaders searched for alternative energy sources. Natural gas became the main fuel for electricity in the 1970s. Nuclear power plants became a more common source of energy as well. By the early 1980s, nuclear power provided nearly a third of Japan's electricity.

Japanese Successes and Struggles in the 1970s

By the mid-1970s, Japan had recovered from the recession. The economy grew at a rate of 5 percent per year, which was higher than in other countries. Japan became the strongest economic power in Southeast Asia. After World War II, Japan had been required to pay Southeast Asian countries for war damages. Instead of paying those debts with money, it paid them with goods such as radios, televisions, and cars. These payments became advertisements for the quality of Japanese goods. By the mid-1970s, the countries who received these payments had become some of Japan's best customers.

The Japanese benefited from many of the gains they had made since 1945.

They were ranked as the most educated people in the world by the 1970s. Their health had improved so much that women's life expectancies had risen from age 54 to age 75. Men's life expectancies had increased from age 50 to around age 75. Japanese children grew taller than previous generations, because they consumed more meat and dairy products.

Despite these gains, uncertainty about the future weighed heavily on many Japanese people, who felt that their lives were not improving. The cost of living in Japan continued to rise. High housing prices forced most Japanese in Tokyo and other cities to live in tiny apartments. Tokyo became especially expensive. By the end of the 1970s, Tokyo was the most expensive place to live in the world. As a result, people began to question the LDP's ability to govern Japan. The government and LDP leaders faced more criticism than ever before.

Corruption in Government

After a rocky period in dealings with the United States, the Japanese hoped for calmer business and political climates. Instead, they faced problems within their own government when a scandal involving the nation's prime minister came to light.

In 1974, Prime Minister Tanaka Kakuei was forced to resign because he had used dishonest practices to build support for his election and for his business. In 1976, authorities arrested him

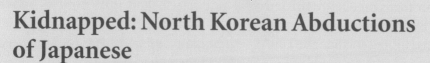

Kidnapped: North Korean Abductions of Japanese

In 2002, the North Korean government admitted that its agents had kidnapped thirteen Japanese people in the 1970s and 1980s. The North Koreans said they wanted these people to train Korean spies in the Japanese language. They allowed five of the people to return to Japan in 2002 but insisted that the eight others were dead. The Japanese government maintained that even more people had been kidnapped. In 2006, Japan continued to press for explanations about the kidnap-

pings: "We…firmly demand that North Korea return any survivors, disclose the truth about the abductions and hand over any suspects."[1]

The kidnappings became a sore point between the two countries. In 2007, Japanese officials refused to take part in an energy assistance program for North Korea. Several countries offered the program in exchange for North Korea's promise to stop its work on nuclear weapons. Japanese leaders refused to provide energy assistance to North Korea until they got answers to their questions about the abductions.

[1]Quoted in Associated Press, "Japan presses N. Korea on abductions," *International Herald Tribune*, February 1, 2006, www.iht.com/articles/2006/02/01/news/japan.php ?rss (accessed April 8, 2007).

Two of the returned abductees, Yasushi Chimura (left) and Fukie Hamamoto (right), spoke to reporters in 2002.

and charged him with bribery. Lockheed Corporation, a U.S. company, had given millions of dollars to Tanaka and other LDP politicians in exchange for the purchase of Lockheed military planes. The news weakened public support for the LDP.

Japanese Cars Become World Favorites

Production of cars in Japan increased dramatically in the 1970s. From the mid-1970s to the late 1980s, annual car production rose from about 7 million to about 13 million.

This increase in production matched

Between 1970 and 1980, the number of Japanese cars exported to the United States more than quadrupled.

an increase in the popularity of Japanese cars. Japanese cars became popular for a number of reasons. They were well made. They were less expensive than many of their European and U.S. counterparts. They got better gas mileage than many U.S. and European cars, as well.

Toyota, for example, had faced bankruptcy in the late 1940s. Then, during the Korean War, the United States ordered trucks from the company. The orders helped Toyota stay in business and launched it toward future growth. By the 1970s, Toyota was a major automaker. Its exports went from 5 million in 1975 to 10 million in 1979. In the 1970s, Toyota became the best-selling foreign car in the United States.

The success of the Japanese auto industry was in part linked to the structure of the car companies. Instead of making everything themselves, Japanese automakers hired smaller companies to make parts. These companies worked closely with the automakers to maintain high standards of quality. Many small companies might work for a large manufacturer. At least two hundred smaller companies, for example, supplied auto parts to Toyota.

Japanese Success Linked to Fuel Efficiency

Customers in the United States liked the

A National Hero

In the 1970s, Japan experienced a surge in national pride and interest in Japanese traditions. Most people were pacifists (against war), but some admired Japan's militaristic past. This group demanded a change in the constitution to allow a return of the military. They favored a return of the emperor as spiritual and political leader of Japan as well.

Japan's former military force, the Imperial Army, had a strong code. It called for allegiance to the emperor. In 1972, Yokoi Shoichi, a Japanese soldier, was found in the jungles of Guam, a Pacific island. Japan had occupied Guam during World War II. Yokoi had hidden since 1944. He refused to surrender because of the military code. Upon arriving back in Japan, Yokoi said, "It is with much embarrassment that I return."[1] He explained, "We Japanese soldiers were told to prefer death to the disgrace of getting captured alive."[2] Yokoi's story of survival and his loyalty to the military code made him a national hero.

[1] Quoted in CNN Interactive World News, "Japan's WWII 'no surrender' soldier dies," CNN.com, September 23, 1997, www.cnn.com/WORLD/9709/23/japan.straggler/index.html (accessed April 10, 2007).

[2] Quoted in Government of Guam, "Yokoi: The World War II Straggler," http://ns.gov.gu/scrollapplet/sergeant.html (accessed April 10, 2007).

Yokoi Shoichi became a symbol of the traditional soldier's loyalty to Japan.

smaller, fuel-efficient cars produced by Toyota and other Japanese automakers. Interest in Japanese cars started to rise in the United States after the first oil price increases in 1973 and 1974. Further increases in 1979 and 1980 caused fuel shortages. The price of gasoline in the United States nearly doubled. Sales of energy-efficient Japanese cars rose sharply, while sales of U.S. cars declined. The number of Japanese cars shipped to the United States went from about 381,000 in 1970 to about 2 million in 1980.

Automakers in the United States worried about losing customers. U.S. cars were large and got poor gas mileage. The automakers were unable to quickly shift to making smaller, more fuel-efficient cars. As a result, they demanded that the U.S. government make it more difficult for Japanese cars to be shipped to the United States. In a 1980 campaign speech, presidential candidate Ronald Reagan expressed his support of U.S. automakers:

> There is a place where government can be legitimately involved—and this is where I think government has a role it has shirked so far—and that is to convince the Japanese one way or another, and in their own best interest, the deluge of cars into the United Stated must be slowed while our industry gets back on its feet.[10]

Reagan and other leaders believed that U.S. automakers needed protection from Japanese competitors. The U.S. auto industry had struggled during the 1970s. Many jobs had been cut, and people wanted the unemployed workers to get their jobs back. As a result, U.S. leaders began working with Japanese leaders to reduce Japanese car sales in the United States.

Made in Japan

Japanese automobiles and electronics changed world opinions about Japanese products. The label "Made in Japan" no longer meant cheap, poor-quality goods. Instead, this label meant low-priced, high-quality goods. The popularity of Japanese products led to more tension between the United States and Japan. Many U.S. government and business leaders complained that the Japanese used unfair business practices.

Conclusion

In the 1970s, an oil crisis thrust Japan into its worst recession in years. The nation recovered quickly, but the cost of living continued to rise. The Japanese were uncertain about their economic stability. Despite these concerns, the economy kept growing. The need for economic efficiency led to an increase in innovations, which increased the worldwide popularity of Japanese products. The label "Made in Japan" became a symbol of quality.

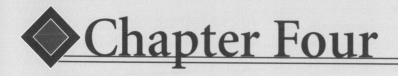

Chapter Four

Japan, Inc.: The 1980s

By the start of the 1980s, countries around the world were impressed by Japan's rise from the devastation of war to the world's second-largest economy. Japan's success was due in part to the Japanese people's hard work, good education, and ingenuity. Employees worked long hours and were deeply loyal to their companies.

The path to success in the business world was easier for men than for women. Japanese society typically expected all women to stay home and raise children. In the 1980s, however, more women chose to pursue careers. Over time, the emphasis on hard work took its toll. Fathers rarely saw their wives and children. Workers suffered health problems from stress.

The trade imbalance between the United States and Japan continued to grow. It became an increasing source of friction between the two countries and even led to attacks against Asians in the United States.

Rise of the Salary Man

The nickname "salary man" was given to a male worker who earned a salary in a white-collar office job. A white-collar job is one that does not require wearing work-clothes, such as those of a carpenter or factory worker. In the 1980s, a salary man in Japan typically wore a white shirt and tie to work. Salaried workers had jobs in large corporations, insurance companies, banks, and other offices. The average income for most white-collar workers in top positions was about three times more than the income for young factory workers.

Most salary men were well educated. Generally, a salary man joined a company right after college and stayed with that company for his entire career. Salary men enjoyed a guarantee of lifetime employment, but they had to work long hours and be completely loyal to the company. At large corporations, salary men began their jobs with low pay. Over time, they

In the 1980s, Japanese workers in office jobs made three times more money than factory workers.

worked their way into positions of greater responsibility. With each promotion, they earned more money. As a result, workers who had been at the company the longest typically got paid the most.

To many Japanese, the life of a salary man was ideal. Respect for the position started before World War II, when few people had access to high-paying corporate jobs. After the war, more positions became available and many people wanted them. Parents wanted their sons to become salary men and wanted their daughters to marry salary men. Some workers who wanted to become salary men wore white shirts and ties to their jobs rather than work clothes. They hoped that doing so would get them more respect.

The salary man was expected to make work his top priority. On weeknights, he

Most young men in Japan aspired to be salary men. Some factory workers even wore shirts and ties to work so they would command the same respect as a salary man.

stayed late at the office or went out with company co-workers. He often worked all weekend. Salary men were proud of their devotion to work, even though it left little time for their families. They were eager to help to rebuild their country. A bank worker from the time said:

> It's my generation that built Japan.... I still remember those days of hardship after the war, when I was a child. My generation wanted to escape that low level of existence— that was the driving force of Japan's development.[11]

Night Work

Business outings in the evening were called night work. Salary men were expected to join co-workers at clubs and restaurants in the evening to drink, eat, and socialize. The goal was to create stronger connections among the workers in a company. Sometimes the meetings included men from another company. When workers from different companies met, the goal was to establish a good feeling between the two groups so that they would want to do business with each other.

Night work had an effect on family life

Capsule hotels became popular in the early 1980s. These hotels gave businessmen a cheap and convenient place to sleep when they worked late at the office.

in Japan. Because a salary man was expected to either work at night or meet with his co-workers, he rarely saw his family in the evening.

Death from Overwork

Some salary men were said to have worked so hard that they died. This phenomenon is known as *karoshi*, which means "death from overwork." Stress from working long hours can cause serious medical problems. In the 1980s, stories about karoshi became more frequent. Reports of death from overwork reached into the thousands.

Some people believe karoshi is rooted in historical factors. After World War II, wages were low and the Japanese had to work long hours to afford basic items such as food and clothing. Later, under the system of lifetime employment, the number of hours a person worked reflected that person's loyalty to the company. Hours worked were a factor in earning promotions as well. People wanted to work long hours to show what good employees they were. Some worked more than their bodies could handle.

In 1987, the Japanese government changed the labor standards law to reduce the work week from 48 hours to 40 hours. Many salary men worked well beyond 40 hours per week. One study said karoshi victims had been working more than 3,000 hours per year. This is nearly 60 hours per week.

The Business Novel

Most salary men had little leisure time, but like other Japanese, they were avid readers. One type of book that was pop-

Manga Explains the Economy

Japanese comic books called *manga* had been popular in Japan since the 1800s. In more recent times, manga were used to explain Japan's new constitution in 1947. They were used again to explain the Japanese economy in the 1980s.

Author Shotaro Ishinomori wrote a manga about the difficulties of life in Japan in the 1970s and 1980s. It was called *An Introduction to Japanese Economics—the Comic Book*. This manga explained the economics of the time. It included graphs and charts to help people understand complex issues, such as the national debt, the changing value of the yen, and the oil crisis. The comic book showed how the Japanese people struggled with uncertainty in the 1970s and the 1980s.

ular among salary men was the business novel. These stories described the challenges that business people were facing in Japan in the 1980s. The characters resembled real business people. Some tales included romance. Business novels became a source of information about the economic and social issues faced by the salary man and other people in Japanese society.

The Japanese Drive for Higher Education

The route to a salary-man position was a university education. Graduation from a top university helped ensure a salaried position at a good company. As a result, competition to get into prestigious universities was fierce.

To help give their children a competitive edge, parents sent their sons and daughters to special tutoring classes called *juku*, or cram schools. These classes were held after school and on weekends. They helped students prepare for entrance exams to high schools and universities. In the 1980s, students in their last years of elementary school might spend two to three hours in juku classes after a regular school day.

Japanese families valued education for girls as well as boys. Males, however, typically completed more schooling than females. Most women trained for secretarial work or attended two-year junior colleges. Few attended four-year universities, like men.

Women and the Economic Miracle

After leaving school, most unmarried women lived with their parents. It was considered improper for a young woman to live alone. With few expenses, many unmarried women spent much of their income on consumer goods.

When women married and had children, they often left their jobs to care for their homes and families. One sign of a family's financial position was that the wife did not have to work to supplement her husband's income. If her husband was a successful salary man, he would earn enough money to support the family.

Changing Attitudes about Work and Family in the 1980s

In the 1980s, more educated women entered the workforce intending to stay in their jobs longer. Many married later and decided to have only one or two children. Japan's cost of living was too high to support a large family.

Some women returned to the workforce after their children went to school. They often had difficulty getting good full-time work. Many were forced to take part-time and temporary jobs. These

In the 1980s, many young children would spend up to three hours after school improving their academic skills in juku, or cram classes.

The 1986 Equal Opportunity Employment Law gave Japanese women the same opportunities in the workforce as men.

positions did not pay well, but companies favored them as a way to lower business costs. By the late 1980s, women made up more than 40 percent of the total workforce. Most of the jobs, however, were part-time. Typical positions for women included office work such as filing and typing, factory work, and retail work in grocery and clothing stores.

Not all members of Japanese society favored working women. Many business owners and families expected a woman to quit her job when she married. Women often felt pressured to leave the workplace. Even well-educated women had trouble getting good jobs. Many employers thought that a woman would leave the company after a few years to get married and have children. Those employers typically did not give women jobs that led to management positions. Some people also believed that giving a job to a woman took away a job from a man.

The Wage Gap

In 1986, Japan enacted the Equal Opportunity Employment Law. The law's purpose was to give women the same opportunities as men to get good jobs and pay. Government leaders wanted to discourage companies from pressuring women to leave their jobs when they got married or became pregnant. The law required businesses to hire and promote women in a manner equal to that of men.

In practice, however, women's wages and chances for promotion did not equal those of men. Women made about one-half to two-thirds as much as men in the late 1980s. Part of the reason for the wage gap was because of the traditional Japanese payment system. In this system, younger workers began at low wages and received pay increases with each promotion over time. By leaving the workforce to have children, women lost their seniority, or built-up time. When they came back to work, they had to start over at the pay rate of much younger workers.

In recent years, however, Japanese women have moved into positions with greater responsibility and higher pay. More women are now working as corporate managers, doctors, and high-ranking government officials. Some Japanese women have chosen to take jobs with foreign companies, which they find offer more opportunities for promotion.

Declining Birth Rate

Japan's birth rate began to fall in the 1960s. By the 1980s, the rate had fallen so far that the population was decreasing. Some men and government leaders blamed women for this drop. In 1990, one leader expressed concern about women who worked:

> There is now a mood [in Japan] to enjoy life, rather than giving birth.... Many Japanese women have entered university and taken a job that will lead them to marry late and have a shorter time for having babies.[12]

This government official blamed working women for the declining birth rate.

The M-Curve

The M-Curve is a type of graph that looks like the letter *M*, with two peaks. This M-Curve shows the ages at which Japanese women typically work. According to the graph, after World War II, most Japanese women worked until about their mid-twenties, when they married and had children. These women then went back to work after raising their children. By this time, they were in their forties. Graphs of working women in the United States and Europe do not show the same sharp drop in the female workforce.

The number of women who continue to work through their twenties and thirties has increased in Japan in recent years. This trend is due to the fact that many women are waiting until their thirties to marry, and they have children later in life. Some women continue to work even with children in the home.

Studies, however, showed that working women were not having fewer children than nonworking women. All families in Japan were having fewer children.

Trade Wars

A trade imbalance between Japan and the United States became a growing source of friction between the two countries in the 1980s. The imbalance meant that Japan was selling more goods in the United States than the United States was selling in Japan. According to the U.S. government, the imbalance ballooned from $10 billion in 1980 to about $50 billion in the late 1980s. In other words, Japanese companies were selling about $50 billion more in products to the United States than U.S. companies were selling to Japan.

Most of Japan's exports in the 1980s were machines. They included cars, small appliances, and electronics such as calculators, copy machines, and video players. Such items made up more than 70 percent of Japan's exports. Japan became the world's leading exporter of semiconductors. A semiconductor is a material used in electronic devices, including computers, cars, and calculators. U.S. companies once had been the leading producers of such goods. Leaders of these companies resented losing sales to Japanese businesses.

Action on the Japanese Auto Industry

The trade imbalance brought action from the U.S. government. A main area of concern was the automobile industry. U.S. automakers claimed that Japanese companies were artificially lowering the cost of their cars in the United States.

Few U.S. automobiles were sold in Japan in the 1980s. Total imports of foreign automobiles into Japan never went above 60,000 vehicles per year between 1945 and 1985. Experts found that U.S. automakers were losing sales largely because their cars were not as efficient as Japanese cars. Nonetheless, the U.S. government pressured Japan to limit its car shipments to the United States.

In 1981, Japan agreed to limit its shipments to the United States to 1,680,000 vehicles. The limit was raised to 2,300,000 vehicles in 1985 and remained in effect for the rest of the decade. Although the Japanese sold fewer cars in the United States, they began selling more expensive car models there. U.S. automakers responded by raising prices on U.S. cars instead of improving their quality.

Japan Bashing

In 1982, U.S. auto sales were the lowest they had been in twenty years. Automakers responded by laying off many workers. The layoffs came during a recession in the United States, when the number of people out of work was already high.

The automobile industry's layoffs sparked much prejudice in the United States against the Japanese people and their products. Some workers felt that their jobs were being taken by the Japanese. Japan's defenders called such behavior Japan bashing.

Racist attacks against Asian Americans increased. In 1982, a Chinese American man was beaten to death by two auto workers who thought he was Japanese. The men were fined but never served any jail time. The beating and light sentencing caused widespread protests by Asian Americans and civil rights groups.

Japan, Inc.

U.S. companies and the U.S. government charged that Japanese business practices were unfair and that they had led to the huge trade imbalance. U.S. business leaders came up with the term Japan, Inc., to describe the Japanese government and its relationship with Japanese businesses. They believed that the Japanese government helped pave the way for sales of Japanese products to other countries but prevented other countries' products from coming into Japan.

After World War II, the Japanese government needed to protect weak industries while the country recovered. It used tariffs and quotas as barriers to prevent the sales of products from other countries. A tariff is an extra fee placed on imported goods. Tariffs raise the price of imports. Quotas are limits on the number of goods that can come into a country.

For many years, the Japanese tightly restricted imports. They allowed countries to send goods that the Japanese did

Japanese workers were often expected to socialize with each other after work, through activities such as karaoke. This helped develop strong business partnerships.

not have themselves, such as lumber, cotton, soybeans, wheat, and sophisticated scientific machinery. The barriers helped Japanese industries grow after the war. Leaders used laws and complex rules to keep foreign products out of Japan. In addition, social connections were at the foundation of many business deals. Japanese business people relied heavily on old, trusted partnerships and placed great importance on personal relationships. Co-workers and business partners often spent evenings socializing with each other.

By the 1980s, Japanese industries had recovered from their earlier economic troubles. As a result, other countries insisted that the Japanese take down their barriers to imports. To protect its businesses while trying to maintain good relations with the United States, Japan responded slowly. This gave companies time to change their business or grow stronger. When the trade imbalance continued, U.S. leaders pressed Japanese leaders to allow more U.S. products into Japan. Over time, Japan got rid of many tariffs and quotas.

The Japanese Defense

The Japanese defended their success in the United States. Most Japanese thought that they sold more goods due to the quality of their products. In addition, they believed that Japanese workers produced more than U.S. workers. They pointed out that the Japanese had worked hard to sell products in the United States. Businesspeople had learned English, U.S. business practices, and U.S. design needs. In contrast, few

Westerners learned the Japanese language, culture, or practices. Thus, for example, U.S. companies made refrigerators that were too large for tiny Japanese kitchens.

Japanese Action

Japanese companies took action to improve U.S.-Japanese relations. One of the biggest steps was a joint venture between a Japanese company and a U.S. company. In 1984, Toyota and General Motors (GM) opened the first U.S.-Japanese automobile manufacturing company in Fremont, California. The company was named New United Motor Manufacturing, Inc. (NUMMI). NUMMI put many U.S. autoworkers back to work under Japanese management. GM sent employees to the NUMMI plant for training in Toyota methods of manufacturing. Part of this training included working on the assembly line and learning about the importance of quality control.

In addition to joint ventures, Japanese automakers set up their own automotive assembly lines in the United States. Cars made in the United States were not counted as imports, so the assembly lines were a way of getting around the import limits. By the end of the 1980s, all the major Japanese car producers had factories in the United States. The Japanese also built manufacturing and assembly plants in Korea, Taiwan, Southeast Asia, and Europe.

Despite their country's record wealth, many Japanese people continued to feel vulnerable in the 1980s. The oil crises of the 1970s had showed them how much they relied on the outside world for their

The Death of Hirohito

Emperor Hirohito died on January 7, 1989. His reign, which began in 1926, was the longest in Japanese history. Leaders from 160 countries attended Hirohito's funeral. The large gathering showed how Japan had transformed itself from a warring nation to a respected member of the international community.

Hirohito's son, Akihito, took his father's place as emperor. Akihito's succession to the imperial throne marked a new era in Japan. He was a man committed to peace, democracy, and cooperation with other countries.

The name of Akihito's reign was *Heisei*, which means "peace and achievement."

In 1959, Akihito married Michiko Shoda, who was not part of a royal family. This was the first time in Japanese imperial history that an emperor had married a commoner.

Hirohito's elaborate state funeral in 1989 cost $74.4 million.

economic prosperity. Japan faced competition from new Southeast Asian countries such as Singapore. Prices of land and consumer goods continued to rise. Unemployment also rose, although it was still much lower than in the United States.

Conclusion

Japan's economic power continued to expand during the 1980s. It brought success and wealth to many Japanese but led to increasing tension with Japan's business competitors in other countries, especially the United States.

Economic success had some drawbacks for the Japanese people. Men in white-collar jobs were expected to work days, nights, and often weekends. As a result, many children rarely saw their fathers, and some men experienced health problems due to their long hours at work. The wage gap between men and women increased. Many people worried that Japan's prosperity would not last.

◆ Chapter Five

The Lost Decade

In the 1990s, several social and economic problems created new challenges for the Japanese people. A weak economy caused some banks and companies to fail. With fewer jobs available, the number of unemployed people increased. Unemployed workers and Japan's many aging citizens needed assistance from the government. The country, however, had few systems in place to care for them. People began to lose confidence in the nation's government. Then, a strong earthquake shook the city of Kobe, killing thousands of people. The government's poor response to this crisis and the nation's economic problems led to the downfall of the Liberal Democratic Party. Such economic and social setbacks led to the 1990s being called Japan's lost decade.

The Japanese Reach Record Wealth

By the end of the 1980s, Japan had become famous all over the word for its wealth. This wealth came from business successes and a steady increase in the value of Japan's currency, the yen. The yen's value rose more than two-and-a-half times from the 1970s to the late 1980s. As a result, many Japanese citizens were among the richest people in the world at the start of the 1990s.

The increase in the yen's value gave the Japanese more buying power. Many traveled to the world's major tourist sites. They bought luxury items, such as expensive cars and designer clothing. Families bought retirement homes in Hawaii.

At the end of the 1980s, many Japanese people used their wealth to travel around the world.

Japanese companies looked for ways to spend their money, too. They bought land, buildings, and businesses in the United States. The Mitsubishi company, for example, bought New York City's Rockefeller Center. In 1987, a Japanese insurance company paid 39.9 million dollars for Sunflowers, a painting by Vincent Van Gogh. It was the most ever paid for a work of art at that time.

Japan's banks made money every time they helped with a purchase, which allowed them to grow wealthy. By the late 1980s, nine of the world's ten largest banks were Japanese. Many of these banks were in Tokyo, so the city became a powerful banking center.

Negative Effects of the Strong Yen

Not all Japanese people benefited from the strong yen. For the people living in Japan, everything was expensive. It cost more to live in Japan, especially in Tokyo, than anywhere else in the world. Most people could not afford to own a home.

Because of the yen's value, Japanese products and the cost of doing business in Japan were expensive. Cheaper goods came into Japan from other countries, so Japanese companies had to lower their prices to get Japanese people to buy their products. When these companies lowered their prices, they reduced their profits. Lower profits meant that the companies had less money to spend on improving products, increasing production, and expanding business. As a result, they had fewer new jobs to offer.

To save money, some companies moved their factories to countries where it was cheaper to do business. Many consumer electronics factories moved. The loss of factories in Japan meant fewer jobs for Japanese workers.

Risky Spending

People around the world began to view Japan as a place to make money by buying and selling land. Some bought stocks in Japanese companies. Stocks are shares of ownership in a company. From 1986 to 1990, prices of land and stocks continued to rise, and more people invested in them.

Many of the investments were risky. People bought land at extremely high prices. Land prices were so high that the land on which the emperor's palace sat was said to be worth more than all the land in California.

People and companies borrowed money from banks to make these investments. Banks lent money without carefully checking to see whether the investments were worth the price and whether the borrowers could pay back the loans.

In the 1990s, Tokyo was such an expensive place to live that many people could only afford a small apartment.

In the 1990s, the land the emperor's palace sat on was said to be worth more than all of the land in California.

The Bubble Economy

In 1990, the investment boom ended abruptly. That year, the government of Japan stopped the risky spending. It set strict new rules on who could borrow to buy property. The government also raised the cost of getting loans. Prices of land and stocks soon began to fall. The period from 1986 to 1990 was called the bubble economy in Japan because rapid economic expansion came to a sudden end, like the bursting of a bubble.

When prices fell, individuals and companies lost money. Most invest- ments became worth less than their original cost. Many buildings and parcels of land were worth only a frac- tion of what people had paid for them. As a result, some borrowers could not afford to repay their loans. This caused bank profits to drop, and several banks went out of business.

In response to the government's action, banks reduced their lending. Generally, only big, well-known busi- nesses got loans. Small and medium- sized businesses, however, had been the driving force in the Japanese economy.

Japan's Economic Bubble

An economic bubble is a period of time when there is tremendous economic growth in a nation followed by a rapid economic decline. In Japan, the start of the bubble began when the value of the yen increased in the mid-1980s. With the yen worth more, businesses and individuals began investing in stocks, land, and buildings. People profited from the sale of these investments, which encouraged them to invest even more. Large corporations made so much money from investments that they no longer needed to borrow from banks. As a result, some banks looked for other customers. They began lending to smaller businesses and customers with poor credit histories.

Many borrowers used the land or buildings they were buying as collateral for their loans. Collateral is an item of value that goes to the lender if the borrower cannot pay off the loan. After the economic bubble burst, collateral such as land was worth less than the price of many of the loans. This left banks with a large amount of bad debt.

These were the businesses where most people worked. Without loans from banks to expand or modernize, many smaller companies went bankrupt. These business failures added to Japan's rising unemployment.

Response to the Crisis

The collapse of banks and businesses required action by the Japanese government. In addition, business leaders from the United States and other countries continued to press for greater economic access to Japan. The government responded by allowing more imports, letting some businesses fail if they could not make money, and ending lifetime employment guarantees. Government leaders hoped that these actions would help the economy in the long term, even if they hurt some companies and employees in the short term.

Most business leaders agreed with the need for changes, pointing to a successful example of change that had helped the Japanese economy. In the early 1990s, Japanese telephone companies rented cell phones to customers. These phones were expensive, and few people could afford them. When the government allowed foreign companies, such as U.S.-based Motorola, to sell inexpensive phones in Japan, the number of cell phone users increased dramatically. Between 1994 and 1997, the number of cell phone users increased from 500,000 to 24,000,000 people. The sale of cell phones boosted Japan's economic health.

Between 1994 and 1997, cell phone users in Japan increased from 500,000 to 24,000,000. This helped improve the struggling Japanese economy.

Japanese leaders, however, were reluctant to take drastic action to fix the nation's economy. Rapid change was not part of Japanese culture. Leaders also feared that quick changes might increase unemployment. As a result, government and business responses to Japan's economic problems came very slowly.

A Break in the LDP's Rule

Public trust in the long-ruling Liberal Democratic Party (LDP) fell in the 1990s. Most Japanese people no longer believed that the LDP could fix their problems. Some LDP officials became involved in scandals. Investigators found that many politicians in the LDP accepted payoffs from companies and then gave the companies big government jobs. Believing it was time for change, the majority of people voted against the LDP during elections at the end of the 1990s. Koizumi Junichiro became Japan's new prime minister. For the first time since the formation of the party in 1955, the LDP did not control Japan's government.

The Kobe Earthquake

In 1995, a powerful earthquake shook Kobe, a port city in western Japan. The earthquake killed thousands of people and damaged more than 250,000 homes. Hundreds of thousands of people had no water or electricity. The Japanese government responded slowly to the crisis and hindered outside attempts to help. For example, the government refused offers of trained dogs that could help find people in wreckage. The government insisted that the dogs be quarantined for long periods before entering the country. One commentator described the response as shameful:

The worst part of the administration's failure in crisis management was that it 'struck out' without even swinging at the ball. Nothing could be more shameful than the inaction, indecision, and inertia that characterized the initial response of the disaster.[1]

The poor response by government leaders further eroded people's already weakened confidence in the government.

[1]André Sorensen, *The Making of Urban Japan* (London: Routledge, 2002), 295–296.

The 1995 Kobe earthquake killed more than 5,500 people.

Japan's Growing Responsibilities

Even with its financial problems, Japan remained one of the richest countries in the world. In the mid-1990s, Japan produced more goods and services than the rest of Asia combined. Japanese people were generally healthy, too. Life expectancies for men and women were among the highest in the world.

Japanese wealth drew attention to Japan's level of responsibility in world events. Many people in the United States resented the trade imbalance with Japan. They questioned why Japan did not take a leadership role in international affairs. Some criticized Japan for not fully paying for its own national defense, even though the United States and its allies had forced Japan to get rid of its military during its postwar restructuring. Instead of a large-scale military, Japan had created a special police force called the Self-Defense Force (SDF). The 1947 constitution limited the amount of money Japan could spend on this force, but the figure was calculated as a percentage of the country's annual earnings. Because of its sizable economic growth, by the early 1990s Japan was spending more on its national defense than any other nations except the United States and the Soviet Union.

The Gulf War and the Constitution

In 1990, Iraqi forces invaded Kuwait. Many nations around the world, including Japan, relied on oil from Kuwait. Leaders of these nations were concerned about the safety and control of Kuwaiti oil reserves. The United States led an international effort to force Iraq out of Kuwait.

U.S. officials wanted Japan to join the effort. The request set off heated discussions in Japan. Article 9 of Japan's postwar constitution barred the country from sending troops overseas. Some Japanese had long opposed Article 9. They believed that Japan had a right to have a military force. Others strongly supported Article 9 and opposed the use of military force by Japan.

In the end, Japan contributed 13 billion dollars toward the war. Many U.S. leaders criticized Japan for not sending troops. Japanese leaders were frustrated that their contribution was not more appreciated. This incident convinced some U.S. leaders that Japan was unwilling to take a greater

After the Gulf War ended in 1991, Japan sent troops to the Middle East to help clear land mines.

role in international affairs.

After the Gulf War, the Japanese government sent the SDF to the Middle East to help clear explosive devices. That mission was the first time Japanese defense forces had been used outside Japan since World War II. The SDF's presence in other countries increased after the Japanese government passed a peace-keeping operations law. This law allowed the SDF to help the United Nations with peacekeeping and election-monitoring efforts around the world, including missions in Rwanda, Bosnia, El Salvador, and the Golan Heights on the Israeli-Syrian border.

Challenges and Changes in Japan

Japan's increasing involvement in international events was not the only change that Japanese people faced. The Japanese economy caused changes in society as well. Due to the high cost of living, people decided to have fewer children. Some workers moved far away from their jobs to live in slightly larger, more affordable homes. This increased workers' commuting time, which decreased the time they spent with their families.

The divorce rate increased. Some couples were dissatisfied with the traditional marriage that had been arranged by their families. Other couples divorced because they could not have children or could not agree to have children. Children were considered the core of Japanese families. Although divorce had

The economic problems of the 1990s changed Japanese society. Divorce rates increased and fewer people had children.

become more acceptable in Japan, the nation's divorce rate remained well below that of other industrialized countries. For example, the rate of divorce in the United States was twice as high as the rate in Japan.

Many of the changes in Japanese society had begun in previous decades. Some of the changes, however, were relatively new. The rising unemployment rate and the continued sinking of the economy were challenges faced by a new generation of Japanese.

In the 1990s, Japan's unemployment rate rose to six percent. Job placement offices in Tokyo were crowded with people looking for work on job-search terminals.

Unemployment

For many years, Japan had prided itself on its low level of unemployment. Japan had maintained a low unemployment rate from the late 1950s through the early 1980s. After the economic bubble burst in 1990, unemployment rose from 1 percent of the workforce to 6 percent of the workforce.

Unemployed workers included young, old, skilled, and unskilled. Some came from companies that had cut employees to reduce costs. Many were part of the temporary workforce. In the 1990s, companies increasingly hired only temporary employees. These workers could be let go once a particular project was done. Some unemployed workers were from regions where old industries were shutting down. These regions included coal-mining towns in the north and south and coastal areas where steel for shipbuilding was produced.

Concern about unemployment spread throughout the country. Even people who were employed worried that they might lose their jobs or some of their pay. The Japanese population as a whole became cautious about spending money. With people buying fewer goods and services, businesses made less money. This loss of income required businesses to reduce expenses. One way they did this was to cut back on jobs. This further fueled the unemployment rate.

The Issue of Elder Care

In the 1990s, Japan had a growing population of senior citizens. The number of senior citizens rose from about 5 percent of the population in the 1960s to about 17 percent of the population by 2000. In keeping with Japanese tradition, individual families generally took responsibility for their elder members. Most of this responsibility fell to women in the family.

Most Japanese senior citizens lived on their savings. Consequently, they were

In the traditional Japanese family, women would take care of their elderly relatives.

The Asian Financial Crisis

In the late 1990s, much of Eastern and Southeastern Asia suffered a severe economic crisis. Hundreds of thousands of workers lost their jobs as businesses failed. Countries around the world feared the spread of business failures to their own borders.

The crisis happened after a series of bank and business failures in South Korea, Thailand, Indonesia, and the Philippines. These failures caused the value of money in these countries to fall. Some of the failed businesses had borrowed from Japanese banks. When the businesses failed and could not pay back their loans, Japanese banks suffered losses once again. These losses prolonged the financial problems that had started in Japan in 1990.

Although many of Japan's banks and businesses suffered losses due to the crisis, the nation's economy remained strong. Japan was able to promise about 30 billion dollars in assistance to the ailing countries, which was more than any other individual nation offered. International organizations later contributed more to help the troubled countries.

cautious consumers and spent less money than people with steady incomes. Their frugal spending habits contributed to a drop in business activity. The health care business grew, however, due to many senior citizens' increased needs for medical care and prescription drugs.

Housing and care for the aging population became a prominent issue in Japan. Most apartments were too small for extended families. Working people needed help to care for elder family members during the day. The Japanese government set up a program to help fund the cost of in-home care and professional caregivers.

Conclusion

The decade of the 1990s in Japan was a time of economic, political, and social change. Businesses went from great success to failure as the economic bubble burst. The Liberal Democratic Party lost control of Japan's government for the first time since its formation in the 1950s. New social issues challenged many Japanese families, including a rising divorce rate and an aging population. One leading businessman warned Japan to take care of its problems sooner rather than later:

If we take no action and let these problems linger on, the Japanese economy will be headed for catastrophe and will be left out of the world's prosperity in the twenty-first century.[13]

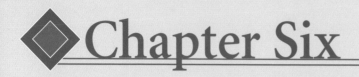

Chapter Six

Japan in the Twenty-first Century

Many of the social, economic, and political challenges that Japan faced in the 1990s continued into the next century. The nation's sluggish economy was one of the greatest challenges. Japanese companies tried to boost their profits by cutting expenses. Some laid off workers for the first time in their postwar history. The value of lifetime employment came into question. Part-time and temporary workers became an increasing part of the Japanese workforce.

Japan's business with other Asian nations continued to grow. Japan faced lingering resentment, however, because of its actions during World War II. The country faced environmental challenges, as well, that resulted in part from Japan's almost blind devotion to economic and industrial growth. Some of these challenges required Japan to cooperate with other nations to find solutions.

Economic Restructuring

Japan's economy remained sluggish at the start of the new century. Companies looked for ways to increase profits. Some explored restructuring, known in Japan as *risutora*.

In general, risutora meant that a company made changes to become more profitable. These changes included job cuts and the end of automatic wage increases. Several large corporations cut jobs and closed plants. In 1999, for example, Sony Corporation announced plans to cut

Urban crowding, as in Tokyo's Ginza district, remained a problem as Japan entered the 21st century.